The Silicon Chip

What is a silicon chip? What is it used for? What changes has it made in our society?

The silicon chip has revolutionized the world of electronics. It has made possible the modern computer and robots used in industry, the programmable washing machine and sewing machine in the home, and special equipment in hospitals. There have been exciting developments due to the silicon chip in space machines, aircraft and missiles.

This book will tell you what the silicon chip is and will explain what it can do. At the end of the book, you can find out the new ways in which the silicon chip can be used, which will make life quite different by the end of this century.

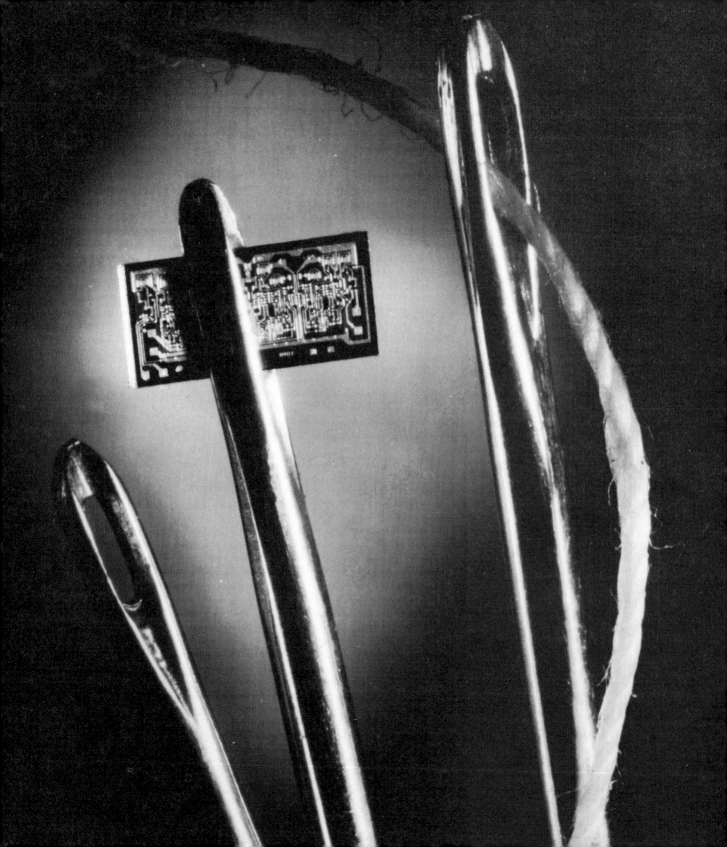

Science in Action

The Silicon Chip

DR KEN WOODCOCK

Wayland

Other books in this series

Frontispiece   *An integrated circuit or silicon chip passing through the eye of a needle.*

Front cover   *To avoid damaging the delicate chips, silicon slices are hovered on cushions of air.*

ISBN 0 85340 758 4

Copyright© 1980 Wayland Publishers Limited
First published in 1980 by
Wayland Publishers Limited,
49 Lansdowne Place, Hove,
East Sussex BN3 1HF, England
2nd Impression 1981.

Phototypeset in VIP Times by Trident Graphics
Limited, Reigate, Surrey

Printed in Great Britain by Butler & Tanner Ltd, Frome and London

Contents

1 Before the silicon chip

(Left) Modern office telephone exchanges contain advanced silicon chips. This helps to make them small and reliable.

Creating a new world

We have become so used to having electronic equipment in our lives that it is difficult to imagine a world without it! How many electronic gadgets are there in your house? You might have a television, record player, cassette recorder, portable radio, calculator, digital watch, electronic alarm clock, electronic camera and flash, light dimmer, perhaps also a TV game and a video recorder.

We use advanced computers which contain silicon chips to work out wages and bills, to help forecast the weather, or even to guide men to the moon! A lot of electronic equipment is used in telephone exchanges, hospitals and television.

But where did all this begin?

A mass of electronic equipment monitors the transmission of television.

Controlling electricity

Man has known how to control the flow of water using a valve or tap for many centuries. By turning the tap we can have a lot of water, no water at all or any amount in between.

Controlling electricity is more difficult. Many people tried to solve the problem, but it was not until 1904 that Professor Fleming invented the 'thermionic valve'. He discovered that electricity could be made to flow in one direction through a vacuum when heat was applied.

Later it was found that while the electricity was in the vacuum in the valve, it could be easily controlled. This was done by putting a wire mesh between the cathode, the place the electricity is coming from, and the anode, the place it is going to. There is a pressure of electricity on the control mesh which is called the voltage. The flow of electricity between the cathode and the anode can be altered by this pressure – so the amount of power supplied by the electricity can be controlled.

Sir Ambrose Fleming with one of this century's greatest inventions – the thermionic valve.

Valves

The first computers contained valves. They were designed to break coded messages transmitted by the enemy and to calculate the paths of shells in the Second World War.

However, valves are unreliable and stop working after a few thousand hours. This may seem a long time, but if there are several thousand valves in a computer, it is likely that one will stop working every few hours. This is a nuisance. If a valve stops working, it might ruin the sum being calculated. It could also take a very long time to find the faulty valve.

Valves through the ages. The one on the left is the earliest.

This type of valve was used in the first computers. It is about 55mm long and 22mm in diameter.

As you know, valves need heat to make them work. If there are a number of them close together, they may become too hot. They are also large, as you can see in the picture. This was why the first computers had to be so much larger than the ones we use today.

Then in 1947, a great discovery was made by three scientists – Bardeen, Brattain and Shockley. They discovered that the flow of electricity could be controlled without using heat or a vacuum. They had invented the *transistor*.

One of the first computers in the world – the Mark I at Manchester University. One of the two equipment racks can be seen here. There are a large number of valves.

Transistors

A transistor is a very small electronic device. Early transistors were made out of a material called germanium.

Soon transistors were made which were much more reliable than valves and very much smaller. Of course, transistors vary in size according to the job they are made for. Large ones control a lot of electricity and may be used in guitar or disco amplifiers. Small ones are used to amplify the tiny signals from a record player or radio aerial. The smallest ones are about 20 micrometres across. Fifty of them laid end to end would

A radio alarm clock containing transistors.

Silicon chips and transistors are used in modern colour televisions. They help reduce the size of the circuit. They are more reliable and use less power than valves.

silicon chips

transistors

A hi-fi system. The sound from the record played on this system is amplified by transistors and comes through the speakers.

measure just 1mm! Large transistors are more than 10mm in diameter.

Besides being very small, transistors are very thin. This makes them fragile. Before they can be used, they are put into small containers which protect them. These can be made of plastic or metal, and if the transistor might get hot, a large metal case is used. Electricity flows through thin wires, which come out of the case and can be connected up by an electrical engineer to other parts of an electronic circuit. Each component, or electrical part, is inserted into the circuit board and soldered in one at a time.

2 The start of a revolution

The silicon chip

There is a lot of silicon about. It is mined in its pure form. Also, particles of silicon dioxide which have worn away from rocks can be found in the sand. The oxygen is taken off by refining, and then we are left with silicon.

So what is a silicon chip? A chip is just a very small, thin piece of silicon with a circuit on it. A circuit is a collection of electronic components, which together can work a machine. The chip is tiny and so the circuit takes up much less room than it does on a circuit board. The machine the circuit is fitted into can also be smaller.

How is this done?

(Below left) Three generations of computer circuits. The old valve circuit is in the background and the small circuit in the front is the equivalent made using silicon chips. The circuit made using transistors is in the middle.

This is the silicon chip before it goes into a protective case. See how small it is in comparison with grains of salt.

thin gold or aluminium wires   silicon chip

pads

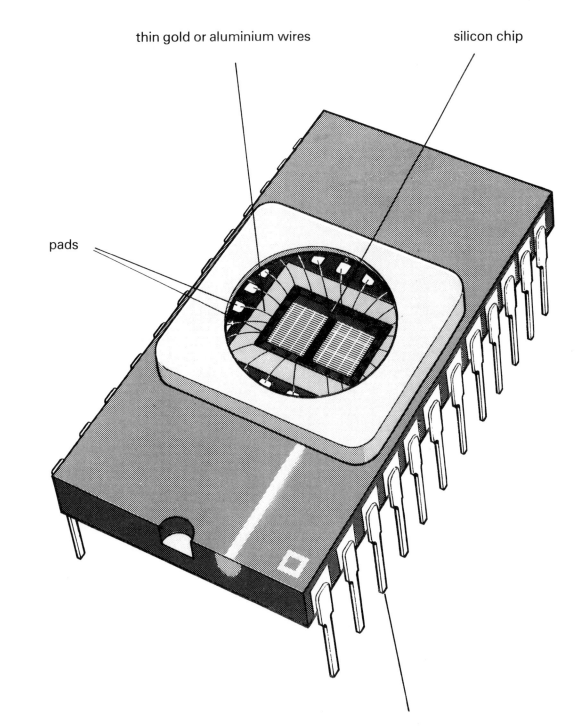

The silicon chip in a case.

thick wires (leads) which are soldered into circuit

Making a silicon chip

Making a silicon chip is a wonder of modern science and engineering! It is made using the purest materials in the cleanest atmosphere. The patterns of the circuit on the chip are so fine that a human hair dwarfs them.

Yet the final chip will cost only a few pence!

Design

The design of a particular chip depends on what it is to be used for. It might be part of a computer, a pocket calculator, a digital watch, a television or something else. The design engineer builds the circuit using transistors and other components to check that it works. If it doesn't, it can be altered at this stage.

Now a diagram is drawn that will be used to replace the large circuit with a silicon chip. The diagram starts off very large so that it can be studied. It is then reduced many hundreds of times by a special camera to the same size as the silicon chip. The circuit can now be put on to the chip in as many as 10 different layers or patterns taken from the diagram.

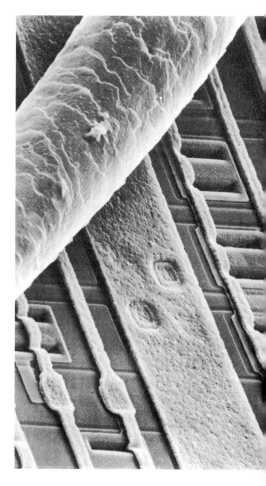

A human hair looks like a log beside the components on a silicon chip.

An electronics engineer studies the circuit built using individual transistors and other components, and draws the diagram of the circuit to go on a silicon chip.

The circuit diagram is drawn out hundreds of times and the girl here is checking each one with the help of a computer.

A computer is also used to check that the circuits on the silicon chips will work properly.

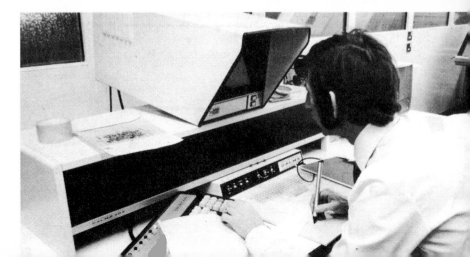

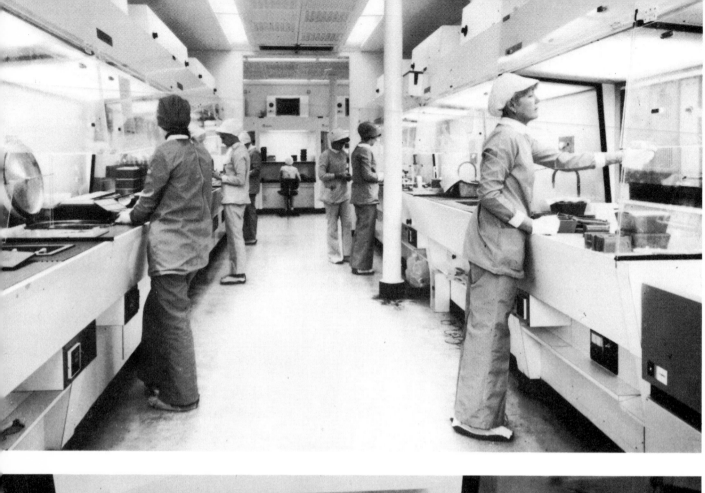

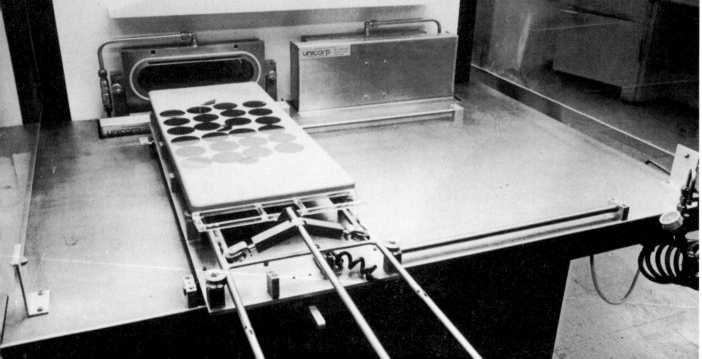

Preparing the silicon

The silicon has to be made very pure in order that it may be made into a chip. In fact, it is 99.9999% pure in the chip. This means that there is less than 5g of impurity in one tonne of silicon.

The pure silicon is made into a rod 100mm in diameter and then slices can be cut off it. A number of silicon chips are made on each thin slice. But first, the slices go into a furnace where they are heated to about 1,000°C. Elements such as Boron, Arsenic, Phosphorus and Indium are introduced. These alter the way the electricity will flow through the chip.

The slices are removed from the furnace. Using one of the patterns of the circuit and special chemicals, some of the surface of the slice is etched away. The slice is returned to the furnace and the process is repeated. Then the next pattern is put onto the slice, and so on until all the patterns of the design are on the slice.

The slice of silicon may contain 500 separate chips. Each chip may contain 50,000 transistors.

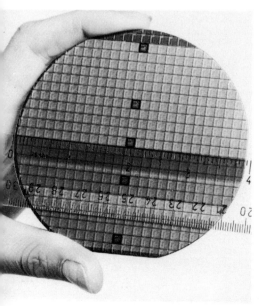

A single slice of silicon, like the 4-inch 'wafer' here, may contain over 500 complex silicon chips.

Packaging

The chips must now be tested to make sure that they are perfect. If any one of the 50,000 transistors in a silicon chip does not work, the chip is no good. To save the cost of packaging useless chips, they are tested before the slice is cut up. A blob of ink is dropped on to chips that do not work.

The chips are then separated from each other with a diamond saw or laser. Chips with ink blobs are thrown away. If the circuit design was very complex, perhaps only one chip in twenty will work.

The perfect chips are put into packages. There are now just two things to be done. There are tiny pads round the edge of a silicon chip which must be connected to the leads of the package. Very thin gold or aluminium wires are welded to them. Finally, the chips are tested again.

The chips are then ready to go into machines. The process of making chips has taken years to perfect. The chips will make a dramatic difference to our lives.

Welding the thin gold or aluminium wires between the silicon chip and the leads. This is quite an expensive process.

(Above right) Circuits that pass the probe test are put into plastic or ceramic packages. You can see a perfect chip on the finger here, and beside it, the packages. A chip is usually 5mm by 5mm, and ½mm thick.

(Bottom right) Very fine probes test each integrated circuit on the silicon slice, as you can see here. Ones that do not work are marked with a blob of ink and thrown away later.

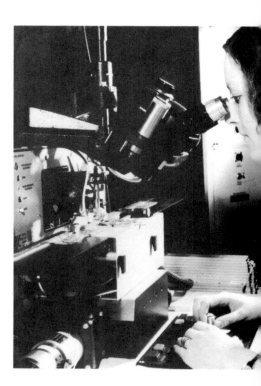

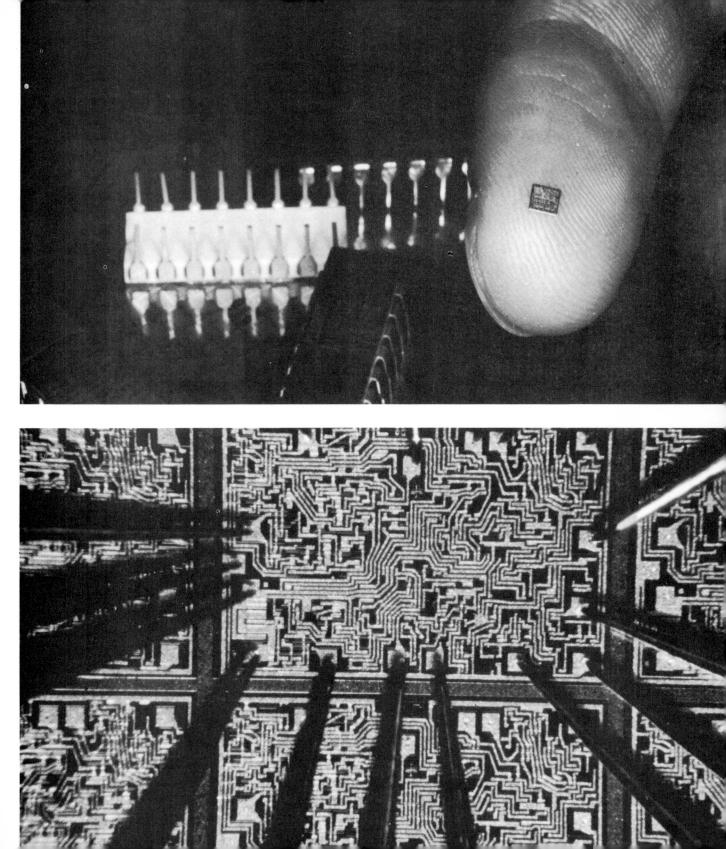

Early computers

One of the first computers in the world was made in Manchester and it started working in 1948. It could do eight hundred additions in a second. Early computers were large because they were made using valves. So that a computer could perform even simple jobs, many thousands of valves were needed.

Early computers used a lot of electricity. Some required thirty kilowatts of power or even more. That's enough to run thirty electric fires or three hundred light bulbs! Nearly all the electricity was turned into heat inside the computer. The early computers got very hot and had to be cooled. This was done by using fans to blow air over the hot parts or by pumping cold water around them. Even today, keeping electronic equipment cool is a big problem.

One of the very first experimental computers in the world was the Manchester University Mark I. It contained a large number of valves and war surplus components.

By 1951, the Manchester University computer had been tidied up. The round objects near the girl's hand are the valves. There were thousands of them in the computer.

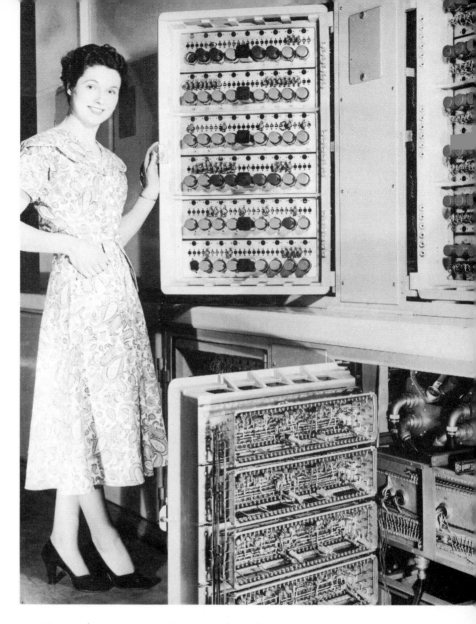

Computers work by obeying many simple instructions. A computer may need hundreds of instructions to solve a simple equation. The instructions can be fed into the computer on punched paper tape, punched cards or directly using a special typewriter. A set of instructions is called a 'computer program'.

Modern computers

Mathematicians in the past never dreamed of doing the calculations modern computers do! Some of the fastest computers today can do over 100 million multiplications *every second*! These computers are very expensive. They are used to perform very complex sums or to do simple ones many times.

Complex calculations must be done when investigating how atoms work. This enables nuclear power stations to operate safely. Landing a man on the moon also requires

Inside the control room of a large nuclear power station. Computers constantly make sure that everything is working well. Any slight malfunction causes the reactor to be shut down.

The possibility of errors being made in the computer can be decreased. A computer which is given enough information can spot that an error is being made.

many complicated calculations. In this case, the answers must be obtained quickly.

Finding out how much money people have in their bank accounts is not hard, but there are many accounts. A computer works out the accounts much more quickly than people could! Electricity and gas bills are all sent out by computer. The electricity and gas men come to your home to read the meter. The numbers they read are then fed into a computer by a person using a special typewriter. In the future, this may not be necessary. Instead, the numbers on the dials of the meters will be automatically sent to the computer along telephone wires.

Calculators

Do you have a pocket calculator? If you have – you own a silicon chip! Calculators were one of the first products to use complex silicon chips. Now, lots of families have one to check their wages or the shopping bill. They used a pencil and paper before calculators were invented! Then they had to know how to add, subtract, multiply and divide. Now they only have to push the right buttons and the machine does it for them.

Some calculators are designed for use by engineers, scientists or businessmen. They do special calculations and can be very powerful. These pocket calculators can solve more complicated problems than early computers.

Thousands of people are employed making calculators. These were new jobs created when the silicon chip was invented. Unfortunately, the silicon chip has made some people lose their jobs – because they made mechanical calculating machines and slide-rules, which are not used much any more.

Many calculators are used in industry. In the past centuries, clerks would spend their whole working life adding rows of numbers. Now sums can be done in a fraction of the time.

This is a complex calculator. It has a number of buttons which you press for the machine to perform different functions.

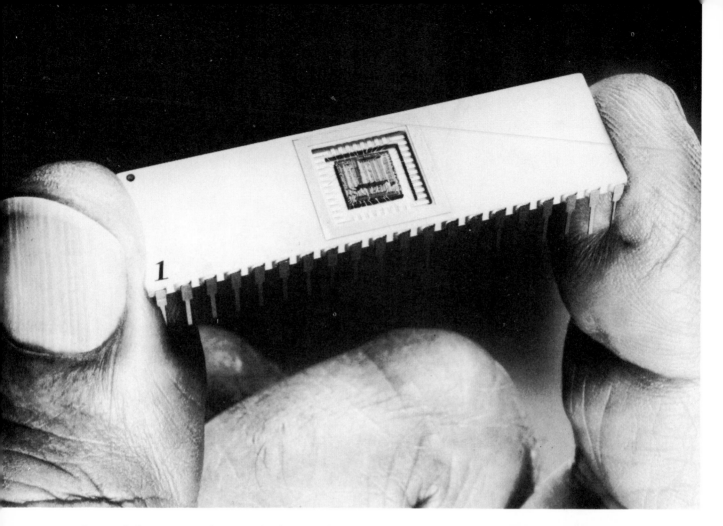

One of the most advanced silicon chips. It replaces a whole room full of valves.

Silicon chips can make domestic equipment, such as this washing machine, more reliable.

28

3 Silicon chips in the home

Microprocessors

A simple silicon chip – one which does not have many transistors – is designed to carry out one job. Some of the new silicon chips can do more than one job. They are like tiny computers which can be instructed to do different things. These silicon chips are called *microprocessors*. They have the power of a small computer, but they are still very cheap.

Washing machines are among the first products to contain microprocessors. They enable the machine to wash better. It will not break down so often because there are fewer parts in the machine to go wrong.

The same type of silicon chip may also be used to run a sewing machine, or cooker. It will receive a different set of instructions. Let's discover the possible uses for such a special chip!

A modern cooking unit.

Sewing machines

Although sewing machines were invented about a hundred years ago, they are still mainly mechanical. Each time a new stitch pattern or technique is added, the machine becomes more complicated inside. Modern mechanical machines contain up to 1,100 parts! Many of these have to be accurately made otherwise the machine would jam. Now, a microprocessor can be used in place of some of the mechanical parts.

The microprocessor in the sewing machine can 'remember' many different stitch patterns. To choose a pattern – you only have to press a button. The silicon chip then sends electricity to small electric motors which make the pattern.

A sewing machine which contains a silicon chip may contain only half the number of mechanical parts of an old machine. It is less likely to wear out because there are fewer moving parts. Many more stitch patterns are available. And the user can invent a new pattern and the machine will 'remember' it. Finally, the machine is easier to use than an old machine. It has electronic displays, which ask the user for information. You then push buttons to select the sewing speed and the number of stitches needed and away you go!

(Right) Modern electronic sewing machines use microprocessors. They can do more than purely mechanical machines.

A nineteenth-century sewing machine.

Information in the home

Have you noticed how much paper comes into your house? As well as the news, daily newspapers contain pages of advertisements. The local papers contain news about cinemas and theatres and many advertisements. Unless you are thinking of going out or buying something, you throw the paper away. Often papers aren't even read.

Silicon chips could help reduce this waste. You could get information by another method. It will be possible to tap out a request for information on a small keyboard next to your television. The information you want will be sent by computer and then displayed on the television. It might be sent by radio waves, just like a normal television picture. Or it could come through telephone wires.

Besides cutting down on waste paper, there are other advantages. The information would be up to date. You could also ask about cinemas, restaurants and theatres in another town. That would be useful if you were going on holiday.

These systems are now being developed. In fact, some simple ones are available now. You might have seen televisions in shops displaying the weather forecast or the latest news. This information is the main programme.

Using a telephone and a modified television, this lady can receive useful information for travelling.

A recipe to try!

TIMES - LONDON TO IPSWICH
MONDAYS TO FRIDAYS
0700 0830 0930 1030 1130
0840 0940 1040 1140 1240
LONDON(LS) 1330 1430 1530 1630 1650
IPSWICH 1440 1540 1640 1744 1806
1730 1810 1840 1930 2030
1843 1930 1956 2040 2152
to return

(Left) There is a micro-processor in this chess set. You are challenged by the silicon chip.

(Below) Use the television instead of a chess board.

(Above) The Speak and Spell machine will test your spellings and tell you if you are wrong.

(Right) Target practice.

Silicon chips in games

Silicon chips can be used to make exciting games! There are dozens of different TV games. Some are copies of real games and sports, like football and tennis. Others are new. There are ones based on battles between spaceships. In others, there are tanks, warships or aircraft.

In many of the games, you play against a friend and the score is displayed on the television screen. Sometimes you need great skill.

Or you play against the silicon chip! Some games are based on chess. Often the microprocessor in the game can be switched from 'learner' to 'good' or even 'expert'. When it's playing like an 'expert', you have to be very good to beat it!

You can also become a marksman. Point the gun at the target on the television screen and pull the trigger. If you are good, you'll score a bull's-eye.

Cameras

Taking photographs is fun. Sometimes though, the results are disappointing. Perhaps the photographs turn out too dark or too light. If you get too close, they may come out fuzzy because the object is not focused properly.

The silicon chips inside a special camera can help here. One calculates the time the film needs to be exposed to the light. If it is too dark, it stops a photograph being taken.

Make sure every picture is in focus! This camera focuses automatically with the aid of silicon chips.

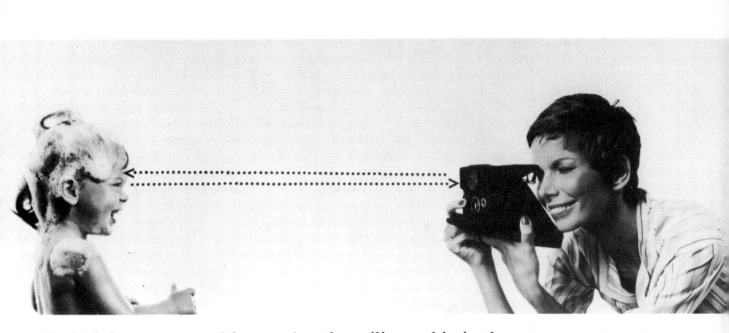

The high frequency sound from the camera bounces off the object. The silicon chip calculates the distance the picture is being taken from.

Another silicon chip in the camera puts out a high frequency sound, which is far too high for humans to hear and even too high for dogs. The sound travels from the camera and bounces off the object being photographed. The sound that has bounced off is then picked up by the camera's special microphone. The silicon chip contains an electronic stop-watch. It has timed how long it has taken for the sound to travel to the object and back again. The silicon chip also knows how fast sound travels in air. It can now calculate how far away the object is.

Another chip in the camera drives an electric motor. This moves the lens so that whatever you have pointed at is perfectly focused. All you have to do is push the button. Of course, you could still cut off someone's head if you are not pointing your camera in the right direction!

4 Helping mankind

Medicine – the X-ray scanner

Silicon chips can also save lives. Doctors and nurses use equipment containing silicon chips to check the health of their patients and to treat them. One of the most useful pieces of apparatus in medicine is the X-ray machine. It is ideal for looking at broken bones and for general examination purposes.

Using a modern X-ray scanning machine, the doctor can examine his patients in more detail.

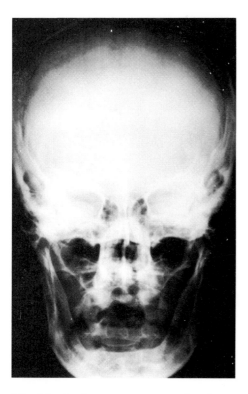

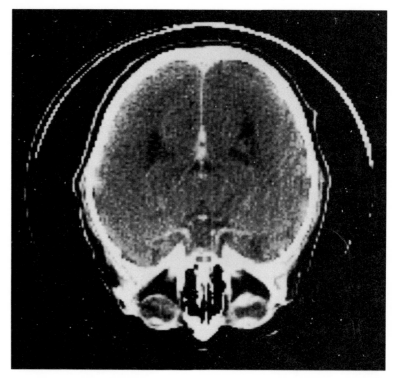

(Left) A doctor cannot look at the brain with a normal X-ray machine because the bony skull absorbs the X-rays.

(Right) But with a scanning X-ray machine, the doctor can see 'through' the bone. Notice the lenses in the eyes. The white area behind the left eye is a tumour.

X-rays pass through flesh and blood, but bones absorb them. So bones show clearly on the X-ray plate.

When a doctor wants to look at an organ which is shielded by bone, he uses a different machine – the X-ray scanner. A normal X-ray machine takes only one photograph, but a scanner takes thousands, all from different angles. These pictures are then processed in a computer. This procedure is very complicated and hundreds of silicon chips are involved. The doctor can then tell the computer to display any part of the body, viewed from any angle. Organs which could not previously be studied can now be seen in great detail.

Medicine – other ways the silicon chip is used

Electronic equipment is at work in an intensive care unit. Here, very seriously ill people are looked after. Perhaps they have had a serious accident, a major operation or a severe heart attack. Wires connected to the patient's chest and other apparatus constantly monitor his condition. The readings appear on a panel which a nurse watches. A change in the condition of any patient is

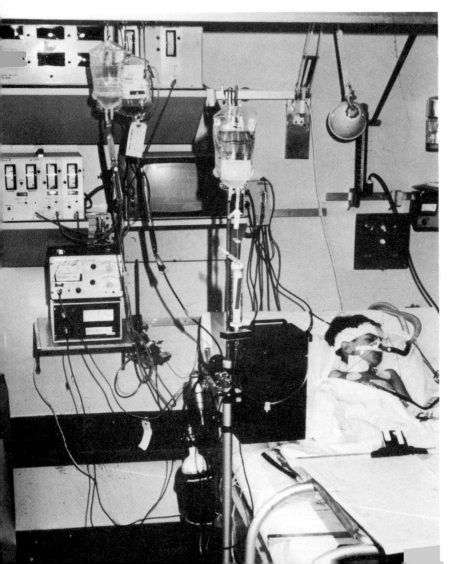

Modern electronics used to monitor the condition of critically ill patients. Notice the pads and wires leading from the little boy's chest to the monitoring machines.

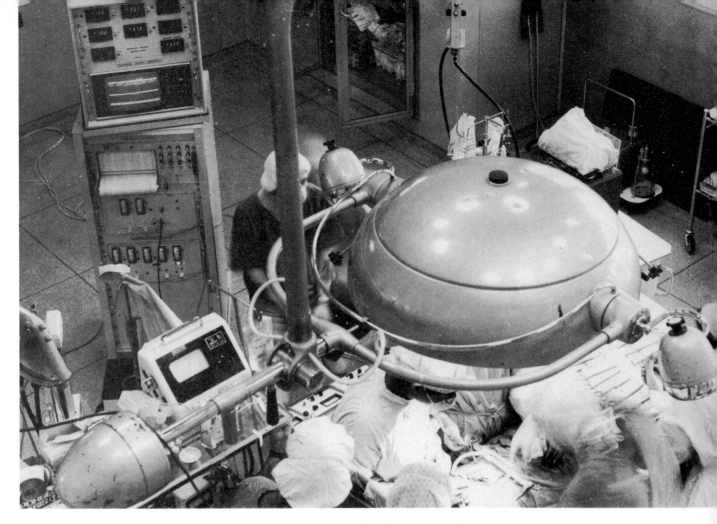

In the operating theatre, electronic equipment keeps a watchful eye on the patient. Any change is instantly displayed.

instantly displayed. If necessary, the nurse can quickly call a doctor.

The nurse probably uses a special 'paging' system to call the doctor. Each doctor carries a small plastic box. It is really a tiny radio which contains silicon chips. The nurse signals him and the box 'bleeps'. As soon as this happens, he can rush to the intensive care unit to attend to the patient.

Silicon chips are also being used to help the handicapped. Artificial limbs, controlled by microprocessors, are being developed.

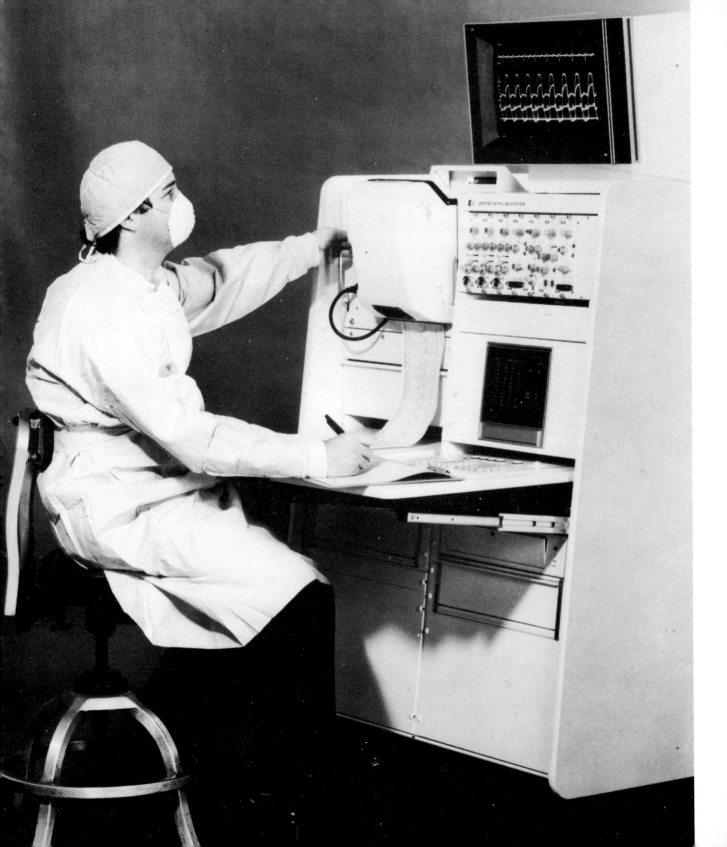

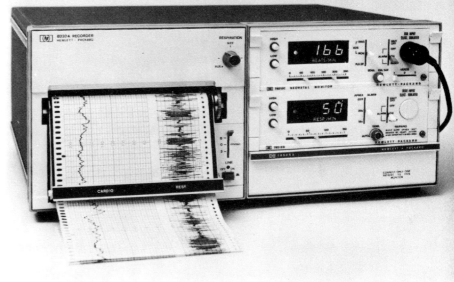

(Left) This machine discovers damage done to the heart, before an operation is carried out. So when the surgeon operates, he knows exactly what is wrong.

(Right) This machine indicates the number of heartbeats each minute and the breathing rate.

Helping the blind

Research to help blind people gain some vision is going on.

An artificial part is implanted in the brain. The implant receives signals from a small transmitter which the blind person can have in his hat, his coat or in his pocket! Connected to the transmitter is a small camera and signal processing unit. The signal processing unit deals with what the camera 'sees' and messages are sent to the brain. In the brain, a small pressure of electricity is applied by the implanted part. As a result of this pressure, the blind person can 'see' a bright spot.

At present, a few dozen spots can be made to appear – enough to make it possible for a blind person to read specially processed letters.

Imaginary robots

We all wish we had a robot! It could do all the jobs we don't like doing. Perhaps it would take the dog for a walk when it is raining or do the ironing. It might even do difficult homework or tidy up the bedroom.

Inventors have tried to make robots for hundreds of years. Some have looked very funny. A few have been useful but most of them have been very simple. Science fiction

writers have imagined very advanced robots. Many of them have looked like humans. They can usually talk and walk. Some of them have appeared to be more intelligent than us. They are strong. They do not have any of our faults. They never forget, can speak every language and can answer any question. All they need is a new battery every now and then – and the occasional spot of oil!

*(Left) Doctor Who encounters daleks, the **ROBOT** which has grown to horrific proportions (middle), and the Robot of Death (right).*

Real robots

The space age robots are intelligent and think for themselves. But even the largest and most advanced computer today cannot do this! All computers do is carry out the instructions that humans have put in. Real robots are nothing more than mechanical devices controlled by computers. They are acting under our instructions.

Real robots often do very simple jobs. They might tighten nuts or weld parts of

This robot is lifting and manipulating dangerous radioactive material. It can left loads of up to 36 kilograms from a distance of 1.8 metres away.

machines together. They do not look like humans. They have no eyes and they cannot hear. They are usually heavy and do not move about. Their arms are spanners or welding torches. The only sound they make is the hissing of compressed air or the rattle of electric motors.

They are an important workforce. They do not need holidays or sleep. They can work where it is too hot or dangerous for a human to work. They do not get bored with doing the same job.

'Scan' is an underwater robot used for inspecting ships' hulls. Scan carries two television cameras, lighting equipment and a stills camera. It makes video tapes and still colour photographs during its inspection.

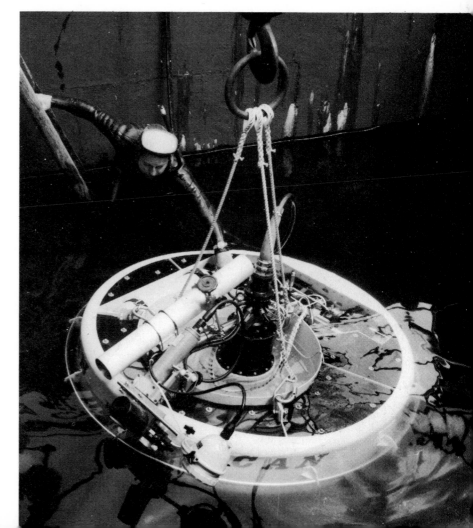

The weather

Some people try to forecast the weather using a fir cone. If the cone opens, it is going to be sunny. If it closes, it will rain. Other people feel seaweed.

Sometimes these methods seem to work. At other times they do not. Even when they do work, the can only forecast the weather in the near future. If we want to know what the weather is likely to be tomorrow, next week or next month – we must use more scientific methods.

Hundreds of weather stations throughout the world record what is happening. They measure the amount of rain, sun, the air pressure, and the wind's direction and strength. Satellites take pictures of the cloud formations. For several days or even weeks, this information is fed into very powerful computers. The answers that the computer gives will make a more accurate forecast possible.

It is nice for us to know what the weather will be like. It can be very important for farmers. In some parts of the world, a forecast can save hundreds of lives. It can give people time to shelter from hurricanes and tornadoes.

The effects of Hurricane 'David' on the capital city of Ruesso on the island of Dominica.

49

5 Off the ground!

(Above) Apollo 11 lifts off. This was man's first landing mission to the moon.

A large computer helping to solve the problems of space exploration.

In space

Landing men on the moon is one of this century's greatest achievements. It could not have been done without silicon chips. Computers played a vital role at every stage. Computers were used to design and test the space rocket and capsule. The computers contained tens of thousands of transistors and silicon chips.

The Apollo spaceship itself contained several small but powerful computers. They had to be small so they could fit into the tiny capsule. They also had to be light, otherwise the rocket would not have had enough power to send them to the moon. They also had to be very reliable. If they went wrong it might mean the rocket motors would not work properly.

Very special circuits were developed for the space mission. Great advances were made in electronics. It is largely due to the space race that we now have microprocessors, digital wrist-watches and electronic games.

Aircraft

Modern aircraft are complicated pieces of machinery. Pilots have to be very skilful and alert to handle them. A single mistake may cause hundreds of deaths.

The pilot has many aids to help him. The instruments in the cockpit convey vital information. For most of the time, the pilot will be watching the instruments instead of flying the aircraft. The aircraft is being flown by a computer called an *autopilot*. This contains silicon chips. The autopilot makes sure that the aircraft is flying at the correct height and in the right direction. If a strong wind is blowing, it takes this into account. The autopilot can even take off and land.

(Left) The skies are becoming more crowded with aircraft. Making sure that they do not collide requires skill and concentration. Air traffic controllers use sophisticated equipment containing silicon chips to give them information.

(Right) The weapon control radar of a modern fighter plane. The electronics is capable of guiding six missiles to their separate targets more than a hundred miles away.

The aircraft can fly thousands of miles without the pilot making any adjustments. Of course, if anything goes wrong, the pilot can take over.

Most crashes occur at take-off and landing. Many of them happen in bad weather. Silicon chips in more powerful computers will be able to give the pilot more advance information, and crashes may be less likely to happen.

Military aircraft contain a lot of electronics. Some electronic equipment fires and controls weapons. Electronics is also used to confuse the enemy, by trying to jam the enemy radar or send anti-aircraft missiles off course.

Missiles

Rockets were invented by the Chinese hundreds of years ago. They were like Guy Fawkes fireworks. They could not be controlled very well. One of the first missiles was the German V2, built during the Second World War. This could be aimed and flew very high so it could not be shot down.

Modern missiles can fly thousands of miles and hit targets a few metres across. Computers on the missile constantly work out its position and alter the direction of the rocket motors to aim it at the target.

(Left) An advance Phoenix missile undergoing tests. The missile is launched from an aircraft and can shoot down enemy aircraft over 100 miles away. The missile contains sophisticated electronic equipment and radar controls.

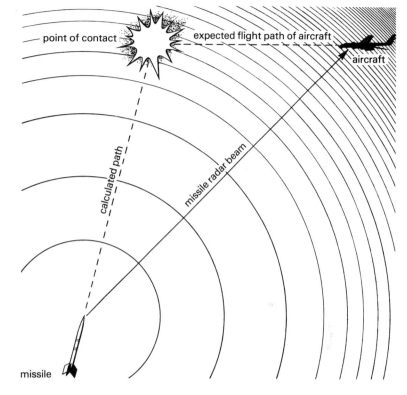

point of contact

expected flight path of aircraft

aircraft

calculated path

missile radar beam

missile

(Right) A missile trying to shoot down an aircraft.

Anti-aircraft missiles are even more complex. Modern aircraft fly very fast so the missile must react very quickly. If it does not, the aircraft can leave it behind or out-manoeuvre it. The missile must find the target using its radar. It must then predict where the aircraft will be in a few seconds' time. The missile aims for this position. If the aircraft alters its course, so should the missile. All the time, the electronics in the aircraft will be trying to confuse and jam the radar in the missile. Which wins will depend upon which has the best electronics. It is a battle between the silicon chips!

6 Into the future

Electronics in the car

The motor car will be changed by the silicon chip. Petrol is becoming scarce and we must use it carefully. A tiny computer will control the amount used. It will calculate exactly how much petrol is needed and then inject it into the cylinders. The improvement in efficiency will make our petrol supplies last a little longer.

It is very difficult to see where you are

A possible interior layout for a car of the future. The read-out of some instruments may still use dials and pointers, instead of a digital display, but they are all controlled by electronics.

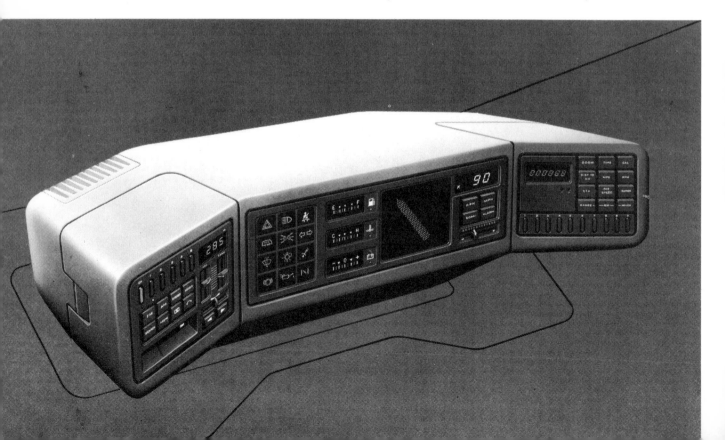

going in a car when it is foggy, raining or dark. It can be very dangerous. Driving may be safer if research going on in America is successful. A tiny transmitter containing a silicon chip can see further ahead than the driver can, and it will calculate whether there is going to be a collision. If a crash might happen, the brakes will be applied.

The car instruments might change as well. The needles could be replaced by digital displays. A car of the future might have a small head-up display. At present, these are used in fighter aircraft. The read-out from the instruments is projected onto the windscreen. The driver can watch the road all the time. He can glance at the display instead of looking down at his instruments.

Here is the new Lagonda car. Inside it has an electronic dashboard.

A desk top computer. Once you are happy with the work displayed on the screen, press a button and it will be printed out.

In the office

Typists spend a lot of time doing things again – either because they have made mistakes, or because their boss wants something altered. And often, the letters sent to different people are very similar. Perhaps only the name and address are different.

Silicon chips can help to reduce all this re-typing. Instead of using an ordinary typewriter, the typist uses a Visual Display Unit – a VDU – and a small computer. The VDU is just a special type of television. There is a keyboard in front of the VDU screen. When the keys are pressed as the

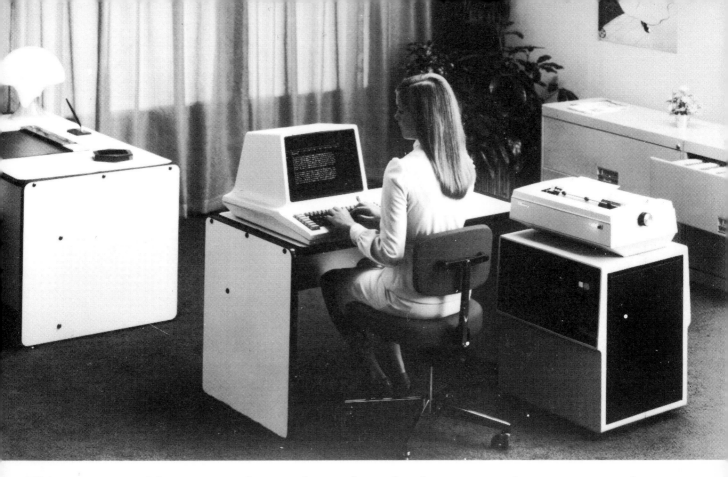

This computer with a VDU used by the typist is called a 'word processor'.

typist writes the letter, words appear on the screen. The computer can write any of the letters or symbols we normally use and it also stores them in its memory. Because there is no paper, the typist does not have to paint out mistakes or start again. She just presses a few keys for letters and words to be inserted or removed, or whole paragraphs moved around. A button is pressed and the letter is printed out on to paper.

Later, if the boss wants to change the letter, it is easy! The letter can be recalled from the computer's memory and altered, using the VDU and keyboard again.

A letter can be stored by the computer for years so it can be referred to when needed. At present, a normal silicon chip can remember about 200 words. Unfortunately, if the plug is pulled out, the words are lost. Special types of chips that are called 'magnetic bubble memories' are being developed. They can store information for years even without power. They will be able to store 10,000 words – many more than there are in this book!

It is too expensive to store letters and reports which are only occasionally referred to. To save cost, they can be stored on 'floppy discs'. These are thin pieces of plastic about the size of a single record. Instead of having grooves, they are coated with the material used on magnetic recording tape. Information can be recorded and altered in the same way as on a cassette recorder.

Much information can be stored on a floppy disc. A few discs could replace a whole filing cabinet! Not only do they save room – they are more efficient. The computer does its own filing. It is easy to find information. To find all the letters written to J. A. Smith, press a few keys and the computer will search the floppy discs and come up with all the letters.

A secretary inserts a floppy disc into a word processor. Several books can be stored on the disc.

(Right) Using a desk computer with a VDU. *A floppy disc is on the table.*

The paperless society

Every year, more trees are cut down to produce paper. It arrives through our letterboxes in many forms. We throw most of it away. The same thing happens in business and industry.

In the future, the silicon chip and computers will reduce the amount of paper used to carry information. We have seen how television and the telephone can be used to convey information. There will be more advances in the field of telecommunications. Letters could be typed on the keyboard and sent over the telephone line, arriving seconds after you finish typing. If the letter was

(Left) More information is being called up on the television. It is possible that newspapers, comics and magazines may be received and stored in the television in the future.

(Right) An alternative to piles of paper. Floppy discs store a phenomenal amount of information!

not important, it could be stored in the computer and sent when it was cheaper – perhaps at night. Bills could be sent in this way. There would be no need for paper.

Newspapers, comics and magazines could be transmitted at night when there are no TV programmes. Those you wanted would be stored in the computer until you had time to read them. At a push of a button, they would appear on the television screen! Pictures could be in colour and the size of the writing could be adjusted to suit your eyesight. When you had finished, the computer could wipe its memory clean. Or you could save interesting parts and make a scrap 'book' of your football team or favourite pop star.

The moneyless society

More people are now using cheque books and credit cards instead of money. Wages are often not paid in cash – they go straight into the bank. People take money from the bank as they need it. They pay bills with cheques. This way, they never have to carry much money.

Gradually, people will use cash less. They will use a cheque, or a credit card. A computer will add up what you buy with your credit card and send you a bill each month. You pay one large bill – not several small ones!

Another development will be 'magnetic

Buying goods in the shops without money. Your card is put through the shop computer which records how much you have spent.

money'. You have a plastic card. On it is a piece of magnetic recording tape on which is a secret code and its value. When you buy something, the card goes into a special machine which records your code and the amount you have spent. Money is transferred automatically from the bank's computer to the shop's computer. Only you and your bank know the secret code, so your card would not be worth stealing.

Something like this will be used for public telephone boxes. There will be no money inside the box so it would be less likely to be damaged by vandals.

Paying by credit card is becoming more popular. People can feel safer carrying less money.

Glossary

Autopilot The piece of machinery that can fly an aircraft automatically. It is a small computer which drives the various mechanical controls of the aircraft. Hence it is a robot.

Computer A collection of electronics which is capable of carrying out certain instructions stored in its memory. If the instructions are changed, the computer will do something different. Hence the same electronics may be used to calculate wages and later to investigate the flight path of a missile.

Head-up display unit (HUD) This projects information onto the windscreen of an aircraft. The pilot does not have to look down at his instruments during dangerous manoeuvres. This may be used in cars of the future.

Integrated circuit A small piece of silicon on which there are transistors and other electronic components. It is also known as a *silicon chip*.

Memory   A device which stores information.

Micrometre   One millionth of a metre, or one thousandth of a millimetre.

Microprocessors   The main part of a computer made using a single integrated circuit. This is a very advanced chip. Usually, it is necessary to use other integrated circuits before it can do a useful job. It is very cheap and is being used increasingly in industry and in the home.

Program (or computer program)   The set of instructions that a computer obeys. For a computer to do a job, there needs to be a set of electronics (called the hardware) and a program (the software).

Robot   When a computer is used to control mechanical apparatus, it is often called a robot. Robots are used on assembly lines and are useful if a job is very repetitive.

Silicon chip   The common name for a silicon integrated circuit. A slice of silicon is carefully prepared so that it is very pure and then divided into tiny parts – called chips. A circuit is put on each chip, layer by layer. A chip can take the place of a circuit board of the past.

Thermionic valve   The first method of controlling the flow of electricity, in a fragile glass case from which all the air had been removed. Using heat, electricity could be made to flow from one end of the case to the other.

Transistor   A small device used for controlling the flow of electricity. It does not need heat or a vacuum to work and is very reliable.

Vacuum   What is left after all the air has been removed from inside an object – nothing.

Visual Display Unit (VDU)   A screen which displays letters, numbers and symbols. VDUs are used to send messages to computers and to receive answers back.

Voltage   The pressure of electricity. A high voltage means the electricity is at high pressure and can kill anyone who touches it.

Word processor   Typists will use a special computer with a VDU instead of a typewriter in the future. It will save the typist retyping a document which can be altered on the VDU screen and the final document typed out automatically.

Picture
Acknowledgements

The author and publisher thank the following for the illustrations which appear on the pages given below:

Access, 65; AMI Microsystems Ltd., 16; Aston Martin Lagonda (1975) Ltd., 57; Barclays Bank Ltd., 64; BBC (& Tom Baker) 44–5; Central Electricity Generating Board, 24; Data Efficiency Ltd., 34 (top); University of Dundee, 48; EMI (Medical) Ltd., 38–9; Ferranti Electronics Ltd., 11, 17 (top & bottom), 18 (top), 20, 23, & 28 (top); Hewlett-Packard Ltd., 25–7, 42, 43, 58, 61; Hughes Aircraft Company Ltd., 53–4; IBM United Kingdom Limited, *front cover*, 6, 60, 63 (right); International Business Machines Corp., 50; John Lawrence, 52; Lintas Ltd., 29; Manchester University, 14 (left), 22; M-O Valve Company Ltd., 10 (right); Motorola Ltd., 19; Mullard Ltd., *frontispiece*; ORACLE, 32; Philips Business Systems Ltd., 59; Photo Research International, 49, 51; Plessey Semiconductors Ltd., 17 (middle), 18 (bottom), 21; Polariod (UK) Ltd., 36–7; the Post Office 33, 63 (left); Servis Domestic Appliances Ltd., 28 (bottom); Singer Ltd., 31; Smiths Industries Ltd., 56; Texas Instruments Ltd., 35 (left); Thorn Domestic Appliances (Electrical) Ltd., 13; United Kingdom Atomic Energy Authority, 46–7; University College London, 8–9; U.S. Forest Service, 62; Videomaster Ltd., 34 (bottom), 35 (right); Ken Woodcock, 10 (left). All other pictures are from the Wayland Picture Library.

Index

Page numbers in italics refer to pictures